Susie Schaefer
FINISH THE BOOK PUBLISHING

YOUR FIRST
BOOK

The Publishing Guide
for New Authors

Your First Book: The Publishing Guide for New Authors
Published by Finish the Book Publishing

SCHAEFER, SUSIE, Author
YOUR FIRST BOOK
SUSIE SCHAEFER

ISBN: 978-1-7353519-5-7 (digital)
ISBN: 978-1-7353519-7-1 (paperback)

BUSINESS & ECONOMICS / Business Writing
EDUCATION / Professional Development
STUDY AIDS / Professional

QUANTITY PURCHASES: Schools, companies, professional groups, clubs, and other organizations may qualify for special terms when ordering quantities of this title. For information, email Info@FinishTheBookPublishing.com.

FINISH THE
BOOK
PUBLISHING

Dedication

This book is dedicated to all the people who have the courage to share their stories and change the world.

Table of Contents

My Introduction to Independent Publishing

In 2015, after a successful 30-year career in Corporate America, I faced my worst fear...going through a divorce with nothing to my name. I moved from rural Colorado back to Denver; working nights at a five-star steakhouse and driving for a ride-share company during the day to give me the flexibility to snap up commercial acting and voiceover jobs as they became available.

A friend who owned an independent publishing company was looking to expand her brand, and needed someone to be her first trained consultant, which entailed helping authors navigate the process of writing, editing, and production of their book. As a book nerd since childhood, I was thrilled at the opportunity and dove in, learning the ropes and slowly building my author portfolio.

When I moved back to my home state of California in 2018 to help my mom through knee surgery, I felt a disconnect with the Denver company. Over a glass of wine with my best friend, we discussed my hopes and dreams, and she said, "Why don't you just launch your own business?" My jaw dropped and I thought, "I can do that?" All I needed was for someone to plant the seed and give me permission. What ensued was beyond my imagination.

As the first entrepreneur in my family, it was a leap of faith - to take my experience, knowledge, business savvy, intelligence, and intuition, and pour it into a brand that reflected my life and my desire to change the world, one book at a time. Today I serve independent authors to help them identify their mission and message by inspiring them to write and publish books that have an impact on the world.

How to Independently Publish Your Book...Successfully!!

Making the decision to publish a book is an awesome goal, so why not put your best foot forward? Getting guidance to launch a solid book will position you correctly for your target market and give you the confidence to become an author.

- ✓ Hire a Book Coach, also known as a book shepherd, consultant, or publishing guide. Book Coaches have resources that are worth their weight in gold.

- ✓ Use a Writing Coach! The first step to keeping your writing on track and on purpose, and helps with accountability, flow of the book, and getting unstuck.

- ✓ Invest in Professional Editing (Development, Copy Line & Proof Editors) – Essentially the first step in the process if you've got a "finished" manuscript, however using a writing coach can be equally important depending on what stage your manuscript is at in the writing process.

- ✓ Create your OWN publishing company, or "imprint," or publish under your business name to protect your

content. Avoid using freebie ISBNs from Kindle Direct Publishing or Ingram Spark.

✓ While in your final rounds of editing, finalize the title and start looking at options for your cover design. Be sure to have your editor review your back cover content to ensure clarity for the reader.

✓ Interior layout includes decisions about headers, footer, chapter pages, font, and images. Note the interior layout, or formatting, is NOT a Word Doc and requires a professional designer.

✓ Proof Your Book! Proof the interior layout, book cover and then upload your files to the Print-On-Demand service of your choice (i.e. KDP or Ingram), then order physical proofs and review AGAIN before "going live."

✓ Prepare for Book Launch Party (live or virtual event) and create your Book Marketing Plan to will promote your book over the next 6-12 months.

Create a Book to Impact the World

Before we get started on the technical aspects of independent publishing, I'd like to introduce you to the idea of social impact or "cause" publishing.

Just think… your book has the ability to make an impact on the world, so choosing your cause is something you'll want to start thinking about early in the process.

Whether your mission is to feed the hungry, save the rainforest, or educate about human trafficking, the topic of your book can help drive awareness to the cause of your choice.

There are a few things to consider:

First, the cause you choose should be relevant to your book's message. For example, if you're writing a memoir about intimate partner abuse, your cause might be centered around shelters or helping survivors.

Second, you can decide if you want a portion of your book's proceeds to fund a cause, or simply add information about how to support various organizations within your book. This can be done in your Acknowledgments, on your Business Page, or even as a list of Resources in the back of your book.

Third, you can also find organizations to "partner" with, by offering copies at a discount, or speaking at events. My recommendation is that you identify small to medium-size organizations, rather than large ones that already have funding and marketing plans in place. The best way to establish a partnership is to contact the organization, let them know that you are publishing a book and ask "How can I help?"

The great thing about publishing independently, is that if an organization ceases to exist, or you wish to change the organization you support, you have the ability to make that revision in your book and upload your updated interior file.

And finally, you can add a sentence or two in your book description that appears on your sales page via Amazon or Barnes & Noble. This will identify your cause to readers even before they've purchased your book. So, start thinking about your book's message and how YOU can have an impact on the world.

3

What Comes First, Second, and Third?

Now that you have your thinking cap on and you're mapping out the plan for writing and producing your book, it's important to understand the timeline for publishing.

Your editing can take 2-4 months, but this is dependent on how much editing your manuscript will require and how quickly you get your edits back to your editor. So, editing aside, let's go over the rest.

There are some things you can be working on in the background when your manuscript is with your editor. You can create your publishing imprint (your publishing company name) and securing a logo, drafting your copyright page, setting up your publishing accounts (i.e., KDP and Ingram Spark), and purchasing your ISBNs.

Once you're into your final round of editing, this is a good time to define your title and subtitle, and get in touch with your cover designer for some samples. There will be a little bit of back and forth, but once you and your editor have a final title, you'll have the foundation as to what you'd like the cover to look like.

One of the most important reasons for using a professional designer is that they understand the types of covers appropriate for different genres. For example, if you're writing a memoir, then the book cover shouldn't look like a sci-fi novel. Just like if you're writing romance, the cover shouldn't look like a business book. Your cover designer will give you designs that fit both the message of your book as well as the genre, so that you'll have better traction in the marketplace. Working on your cover design will usually take about 2-6 weeks.

When your book is finished with the developmental edit, then you'll send the manuscript to a proof editor. Your manuscript should include all of the following elements, including the copyright page, table of contents, dedication, all the chapters and resources section, your acknowledgments, the "about the author" page and, if appropriate, your business page. You'll want the proof editor to see the entire book interior to ensure that any mistakes are caught before going to print. Your proof editor will usually need 2-4 weeks to complete the proof edit.

Back to design...

Now that you have a front cover for your book, you can request samples from your interior layout designer. It's important to have your front cover done, so that elements from the cover can be used in the interior design, such as font choice. There are a LOT of decisions to be made about your interior layout. In addition to fonts, you'll have the opportunity to look at the design for your chapter pages, graphics, headers, page numbers, etcetera. Once you've determined your choices for the interior, the layout process usually takes about two weeks.

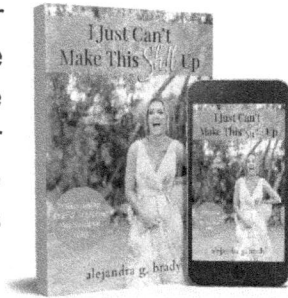

When the layout design is finished, you'll know the page number count. This is important, as the cover designer will need this information to create the correct size for the spine of your book. When you have downtime in the process, be sure to write your back cover content. If your editor is agreeable, I would recommend your editor take a peek at it to make sure it is well-written and in third person (she went to the store, versus I went to the store). Your back cover is a key marketing piece for your book, so it's critical to have a great description that will have the reader thinking "I've gotta read this book!"

The back cover should also include a short, two-sentence bio, your head shot, your publishing logo, and a barcode with readable price. I like to have a header or call-out at the top of the back cover, or use a great testimonial from a reader or someone in your industry.

When files are finished, you'll proof the final files. This can take 2-3 weeks, depending on how fast you are. Here's a tip for you… when proofing your files, read the book out loud (or get a reading buddy), as you'll catch any mistakes missed previously. You'll send any errors back to your designer to make those changes and will receive your final files to upload your book and order proof copies. The final proof process takes 3-6 weeks, before approving and going live.

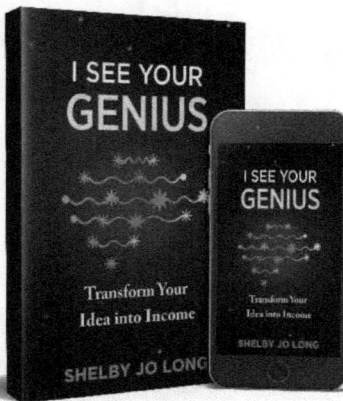

Once your books are live, then it's time to announce your book and plan your launch party. Congratulations! You're a published author!

What Versions Should You Publish? Paperback, hardcover, or eBook... or all three?

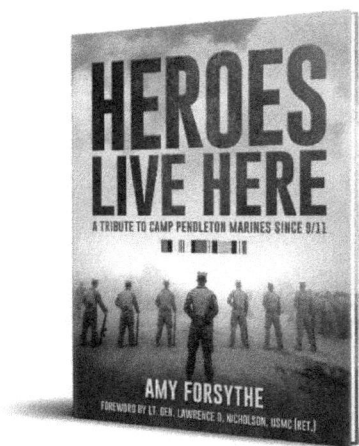

While you're planning the costs of publishing your book, it's a good idea to think about which versions of your book that you want to publish.

Most common are paperback and eBook, however you might consider a hardcover as well. When publishing a hardcover book, you can choose between a laminate cover or a fabric cover with a dust jacket... the choice is yours!

My recommendation is to look at the various publishing platforms, such as Amazon's print on demand service called Kindle Direct Publishing (KDP), as well as Ingram Spark, Barnes & Noble, and BookBaby. There are a lot of ways to publish your book, so it's important to do a bit of research and see which platform offers print on demand for each version of your book. Some may not offer hardcover, while others may not offer full color interior, if that's a requirement of your book.

Typically, when I work with authors, we'll decide which version of their book makes the most sense for them, then I'll recommend the platform that will give them the best results.

For example, when working on a book that has a full-color interior, the most cost-effective option is Ingram Spark. You also have the ability to simply print your books through Ingram and not offer distribution. This is a great option for those doing a legacy book for just family and friends. In addition, Ingram Spark is also the resource book buyers and libraries use, so if you're looking to get your book into a bookstore or library, this is the way to go.

KDP offers their readers Kindle Unlimited for eBooks, which is like a Prime membership for eBook customers. With Kindle Unlimited, authors can enroll their eBook in the program for 90 days at a time. This program is called KDP Select, and customers can buy your book for free through their monthly membership. The benefit of KDP Select is that you still get the royalties based on your retail price, and KDP Select offers promotions to help you market your book. Just be aware; as a requirement of KDP Select program, your eBook can ONLY be published via KDP while enrolled in the program, so there are some limitations, but overall, it's a good resource.

Here's what I do as a general rule for my clients. We publish the paperback and eBook on Amazon's KDP, with the hardcover on Ingram Spark. After we run the Amazon Best Seller Campaign and take advantage of the promos offered through KDP Select, we allow KDP Select to expire, and then publish the eBook on either Ingram Spark or another platform. I happen to like Smashwords, as they have awesome distribution, and since Smashwords is being acquired by Draft2Digital, check them out as another terrific option!

So now you can see why it's important to figure out which versions of your book you want to publish early in the process, so that you can make sure you have included the cost of any platforms into your budget. Ingram Spark charges only $49 per book. There is no cost for using KDP, Smashwords, or Draft2Digital, however they do take a percentage of your book sales in exchange for using the platform.

Parts of the Book

Interior *****Required for publishing***
- ✓ Testimonials or Advance Praise (if any)
- ✓ Half Title Page (just the title - will be done with cover)
- ✓ Title Page ** (like cover - with author name - will be done with cover)
- ✓ Copyright page **
- ✓ Dedication
- ✓ Table of Contents
- ✓ Introduction or Foreword
- ✓ Body of Manuscript ** (your chapters)
- ✓ Resources, Glossary, Index, Appendix
- ✓ Acknowledgments
- ✓ About the Author (150-word bio - more detail about you!)
- ✓ Back Matter (getting in front of book clubs, etc.)
- ✓ Next Book Teaser (if applicable)

Cover
- ✓ Front Cover Design
- ✓ Spine
- ✓ Back Cover

Back of the Book Blurb:
A synopsis with a headline

Author Bio:
Short, 35-ish words

Publishing company logo
Bar Code & ISBN & price

Top 10 Things That Scream "I'm Self-Published"

While many first-time authors dream about getting picked up by a traditional publisher, the process of pitching to a publishing house is time consuming and can be expensive. Many new authors, particularly nonfiction authors who have a business, where a book supports their marketing plan, is a much more feasible way to get your message out to the world.

Some of the benefits of indie publishing is that you get to control your budget, timeline, and your content. You can be off to a great start by doing it on your own, although there are some common mistakes that can make your book look amateur, so check these off your list to keep your book looking it's best.

1. Unprofessional Editing - Not just a proof edit! Be sure to use professional editing services.

2. Foreword is spelled incorrectly. It's <u>not</u> Forward (as in moving ahead), it's FOREWORD (as in "the words before').

3. Acknowledgments spelled incorrectly. Be sure there is no "e" after the "g."

4. Headers and Footers and/or page numbers on your blank pages. This is a big "no-no," but can

be avoided by using a professional interior book designer.

5. Poor formatting, including spaces between the paragraphs, too-small margins, and chapter pages that lack unique or interesting design elements.

6. Not using a book coach and trying to go it alone. Book coaches not only know their way around the publishing industry, they can make recommendations for professional editors and book designers.

7. Ordering bulk print job of 1000 or more books instead of using Print-On-Demand services. Why keep boxes of books in your garage? Order online as needed and ship directly to venues for speaking engagements.

8. Long back cover content. The back-of-the-book-blurb should be around 150-ish words. It should not fill up the back cover. Your author bio should be only a couple sentences and include a terrific head shot.

9. Using the wrong color paper. Yes! There are different colors of paper for the interior of your book. Use cream-colored paper for your interior unless you're publishing a textbook, medical or reference book, self-help, or a business book.

10. Short cuts on your cover. Use a professional book cover designer, not just a graphic designer, as book covers require an understanding for spine

measurements. Your book cover is your only chance to make a great first impression!

About the Author

Known as The Transformational Book Coach for "cause publishing," Susie Schaefer believes that books are the gateway to creating a movement. Her love of books goes far beyond the feel of a fabric cover or the smell of a library. Whether writing a book helps an author heal past trauma or raise awareness for social change, Susie empowers storytellers to be part of the global conversation and create a ripple effect for humanity. Working with business owners brings her tremendous joy, particularly when an author shares their own personal story along with their mission and message.

Susie comes to the table with an array of superpowers; her unique combination of business acumen, street smarts, and mystic intuitive gifts to help people see what's truly possible with no limitations. Her corporate experience working with non-profits, teaching and training in human resources and as a marketing expert, and a stint in radio broadcasting and commercial acting allows Susie to skillfully guide authors through the independent publishing process to finish that dream book, launch a speaking career, or build a business by publishing a book that <u>gets results *and* gives back</u>.

Susie's understanding of social impact, through the integration of cause-based books enables her to offer a unique foundation for authors by building community, creating connections, and serving as a catalyst for change. When not reading, publishing books, or writing award-winning screenplays, Susie can be found practicing her downward dog (yoga), meditating on the beach, or planning her next travel adventure.

Finish the Book Publishing:
>Book Visioning and Publishing Roadmaps
>Publishing Project Management
>Intuitive Oracle Readings & Spiritual Guidance
>https://www.finishthebookpublishing.com/